Rodgers and Hammerstein's
My Favorite Things

Lyrics by Oscar Hammerstein II   Music by Richard Rodgers

Illustrated by James Warhola

SIMON & SCHUSTER BOOKS FOR YOUNG READERS
Published by Simon & Schuster
New York London Toronto Sydney Tokyo Singapore

SIMON & SCHUSTER BOOKS FOR YOUNG READERS
1230 Avenue of the Americas, New York, New York 10020
Copyright © 1959 by Richard Rodgers and Oscar Hammerstein II.
Copyright renewed. Williamson Music Co. owner of publication and
allied rights throughout the world. International copyright secured.
Illustrations copyright © 1994 by James Warhola.
All rights reserved including the right of reproduction in whole
or in part in any form. SIMON & SCHUSTER BOOKS FOR YOUNG READERS
is a trademark of Simon & Schuster.
The text for this book is set in 17.5-point New Baskerville.
The illustrations were done in watercolor.
Manufactured in the United States of America.

10 9 8 7 6 5 4 3 2 1

Library of Congress Cataloging-in-Publication Data
My favorite things / lyrics by Oscar Hammerstein II ;
music by Richard Rodgers ; illustrated by James Warhola.
p. cm. Summary: An illustrated version of the popular
song enumerating favorite things, from raindrops on
roses to silver-white winters melting into springs.
1. Children's songs—Texts. [1. Songs.] I. Hammerstein,
Oscar, 1895–1960. II. Rodgers, Richard, 1902– .
III. Warhola, James, ill. IV. Title. V. Title : My favorite things.
PZ8.3.R618 1994 [E]—dc20 93-26116 CIP AC
ISBN: 0-671-79457-4

For Mary
— J.W.

Raindrops on roses . . .

. . . and whiskers on kittens,
Bright copper kettles and
warm woolen mittens,

Brown paper packages tied up with strings—
These are a few of my favorite things.

Cream-colored ponies
and crisp apple strudels,

Doorbells and sleigh bells
and schnitzel with noodles,

Wild geese that fly with the moon on their wings—
These are a few of my favorite things.

Girls in white dresses with blue satin sashes,
Snowflakes that stay on my nose and eyelashes,

Silver white winters that melt into springs—
These are a few of my favorite things.

When the dog bites,
When the bee stings,
When I'm feeling sad,

I simply remember my favorite things
And then I don't feel so bad!

My Favorite Things

Words by OSCAR HAMMERSTEIN II   Music by RICHARD RODGERS

Rain - drops on ros - es and whisk - ers on kit - tens, Bright cop - per ket -tles and warm wool - en mit - tens, Brown pa - per pack - ag - es tied up with strings, These are a few of my fa - vor - ite things. Cream col - ored pon - ies and crisp ap - ple strud- els, Door - bells and sleigh - bells and schnitz -el with noo - dles, Wild geese that fly with the moon on their wings, These are a few of my